TUNDRA

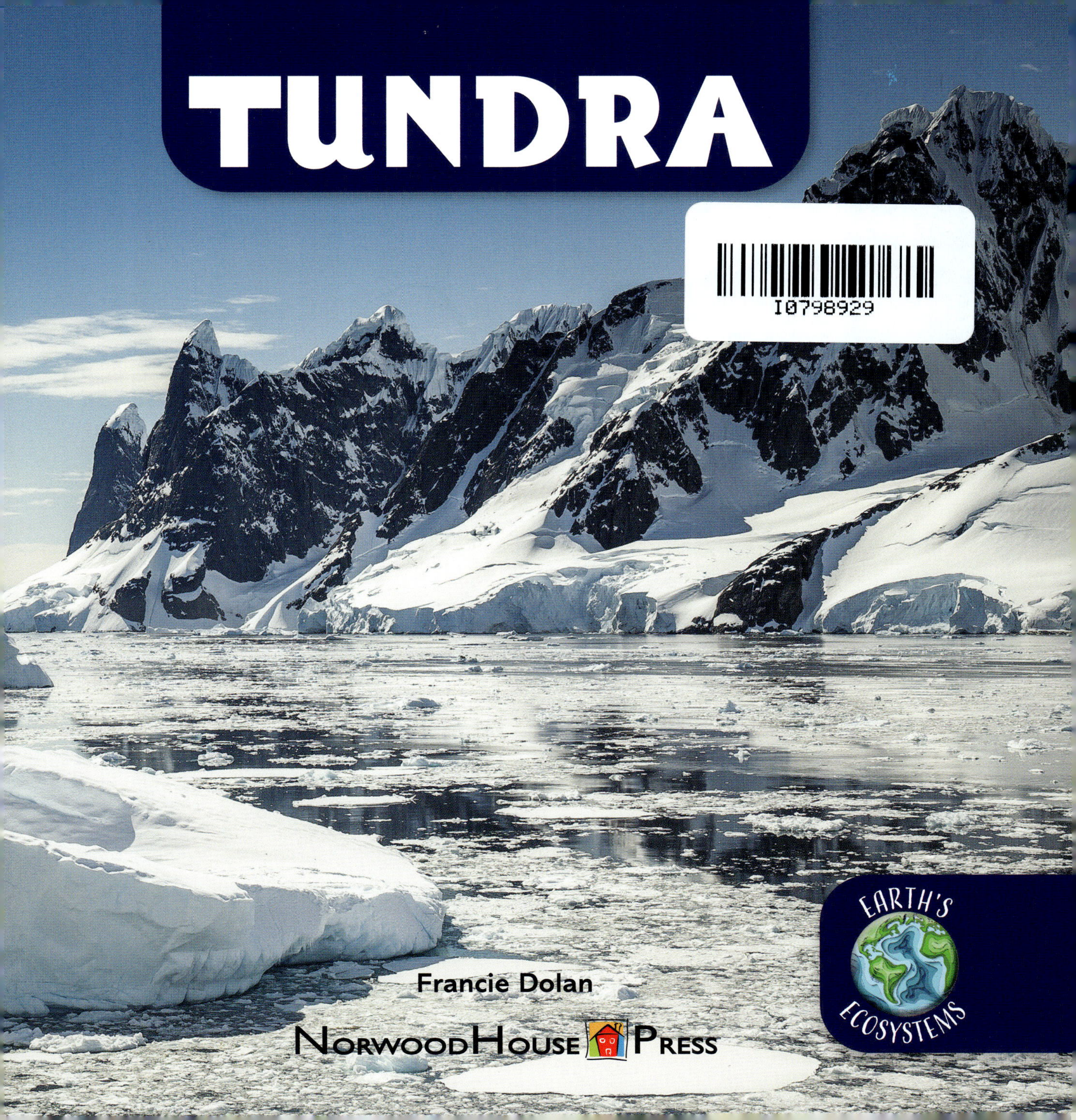

EARTH'S ECOSYSTEMS

Francie Dolan

NorwoodHouse Press

Cataloging-in-Publication Data

Names: Dolan, Francie.
Title: Tundra / Francie Dolan.
Description: Buffalo, NY : Norwood House Press, 2026. | Series: Earth's ecosystems | Includes glossary and index.
Identifiers: ISBN 9781978577169 (pbk.) | ISBN 9781978577176 (library bound) | ISBN 9781978577183 (ebook)
Subjects: LCSH: Tundra ecology--Juvenile literature. | Tundra animals--Juvenile literature.
Classification: LCC QH541.5.T8 D65 2026 | DDC 577.586--dc23

Published in 2026 by
Norwood House Press
2544 Clinton Street
Buffalo, NY 14224

Designer: Rhea Magaro
Editor: Kim Thompson

Photo credits: Cover, p. 1 Lua Carlos Martins, Kumer Oksa-na/Shutterstock.com; p. 3 Troutnut/Shutterstock.com; p. 5 Vadim_N/Shutterstock.com; p. 6 R. Vickers/Shutterstock.com; p. 9 Vladimir Melnik/Shutterstock.com; p. 10 Andrei Armiagov/Shutterstock.com; p. 11 Zelma Brezinska/Shutterstock.com; p. 12 adamikarl/Shutterstock.com; p. 13 Alexey Seafarer/Shutterstock.com; p. 14 Troutnut/Shutterstock.com; p. 15 Nick Pecker/Shutterstock.com; p. 17 Eric Cote/Shutterstock.com; p. 19 Vaclav Sebek, Denis Vesely /Shutterstock.com; p. 20 Egoreichenkov Evgenii/Shutterstock.com

Printed in the United States of America

CPSIA compliance information: Batch #CWNHP26: For further information contact Norwood House Press at 1-800-237-9932.

TABLE OF CONTENTS

The Tundra Ecosystem

Eco- means "home" or "environment." *System* means "a group of things that work together." Earth has many **ecosystems** that support life. Each is home to a network of living things that depend on each other.

One kind of ecosystem is a tundra. It has some of the harshest conditions on Earth. It is dry, windy, and freezing cold. Temperatures can drop to -25 degrees Fahrenheit (-32 degrees Celsius).

One-fifth of Earth's land is tundra, including much of Antarctica and the Arctic. Here, winters last eight months of the year. During the short summers, there is a shallow layer of thawed soil. Below this, the ground is **permafrost**. It stays frozen year-round.

Tundra Plants

No trees grow on the tundra. Plants stay low to the ground. This **adaptation** protects them from strong winds. Most tundra plants have shallow roots. Some have fuzzy stems that trap heat and waxy leaves that hold water in.

The Arctic poppy blooms and makes seeds in just a few days. This allows it to reproduce during the short growing season.

Lichens are a **symbiosis** of two different types of living things, **algae** and **fungi**. Lichens have no roots and do not need soil. They grow on almost any surface.

Reindeer moss is not moss. It's a lichen! It provides food for caribou and other tundra animals.

Tundra Animals

Adaptations help tundra animals survive.

The Arctic fox, ermine, and ptarmigan use **camouflage**. They are white in winter to blend in with the snow. They are brown in summer to match rocks and scrubby plants.

Some animals, like the musk ox, rely on thick, shaggy coats to keep them warm. Other animals, like the grizzly bear, **hibernate** through the winter.

Small animals such as lemmings stay in tunnels. The deep snow provides **insulation**.

Some animals spend only part of the year in the tundra. Each summer, millions of snow geese **migrate** to the Arctic to feed on plant roots. As winter approaches, they leave to fly over 1,000 miles (1,609 km) south.

Tundra Food Chains

In the tundra, living things eat other living things in food chains. An Arctic hare might nibble on moss. A polar bear may catch and eat the hare. After the bear dies, a snowy owl might make a meal of its remains.

All living things in tundra ecosystems depend on each other for survival. These places are important for plants, animals, and planet Earth.

Glossary

adaptation (ad-ap-TAY-shuhn): a physical or behavioral change that helps plants and animals survive in their environment

algae (AL-jee): small plants without roots or stems

camouflage (KAM-uh-flahzh): a disguise or natural coloring that lets animals hide by making them look like their surroundings

ecosystems (EE-koh-sis-tuhms): natural communities where plants, animals, and their environment all work together

fungi (FUHNG-gye): plant-like living things that have no leaves, roots, or flowers; mushrooms and molds are fungi

hibernate (HYE-bur-nate): to slow the heart rate and breathing and spend the winter in a still, sleep-like state

insulation (IN-suh-lay-shuhn): a material that traps heat

migrate (MYE-grate): to move from one place to another at a certain time of the year to find food or other resources

permafrost (PUR-muh-frawst): ground that is permanently frozen

symbiosis (sim-bee-OH-suhs): two living things that stay close because each benefits the other; in a lichen, an alga produces food and a fungus provides a supporting structure

Thinking Questions

1. What is an ecosystem?
2. Where is tundra found on Earth?
3. Give an example of an adaptation that helps tundra plants survive.
4. Give an example of an adaptation that helps tundra animals survive.
5. What does a food chain show?

Index

About the Author

Francie Dolan is continually amazed by the natural world and how Earth's plants, animals, and natural resources are interconnected. From her home near Seattle, Washington, she loves to hike and explore forests, lakes, mountains, and the seashore. When she gets home, she likes to draw and write about what she sees on her adventures.